Quick-and-Easy
Miniature Samplers
for Cross-Stitch

by

Barbara Christopher

DOVER PUBLICATIONS, INC., NEW YORK

To M. C. Waldrep,
my editor, colleague and friend

Published in Canada by General Publishing Company, Ltd., 30 Lesmill Road, Don Mills, Toronto, Ontario.
Published in the United Kingdom by Constable and Company, Ltd.

Quick-and-Easy Miniature Samplers for Cross-Stitch is a new work, first published by Dover Publications, Inc., in 1986.

Manufactured in the United States of America
Dover Publications, Inc., 31 East 2nd Street, Mineola, N.Y. 11501

Library of Congress Cataloging in Publication Data

Christopher, Barbara.
    Quick-and-easy miniature samplers for cross-stitch.

    (Dover needlework series)
    1. Cross-stitch—Patterns. 2. Samplers. I. Title. II. Series.
TT778.C76C476 1986   646.3'041   86-16540
ISBN 0-486-25209-4

INTRODUCTION

Cross-stitch samplers are an American tradition. They first became popular in the eighteenth century as an educational tool, often being the first piece of needlework that a young girl embroidered to perfect and display her stitches.

Today, the sampler remains an extremely popular form of needlework, but the modern needleworker no longer has the time to spend weeks, or even months, completing a single project. This collection of miniature samplers presents over 70 different designs that can be completed quickly and easily—many of them in an evening's time.

The group includes mottoes, traditional samplers, monograms and greetings for special occasions—birthdays, weddings, graduation, etc. When worked on 14 threads-per-inch aida cloth, as those shown on the covers were, the samplers range in size from about 2" by 2" to 3" by 6". These versatile embroideries make wonderful small gifts and can be used for pincushions, canning-jar lids, Christmas ornaments, greeting cards, keepsake boxes and many more projects sure to please anyone who receives them.

These designs were originally created for counted cross-stitch, but they are easily translated into other needlework techniques. Keep in mind that the finished piece will not be the same size as the charted design unless you are working on fabric or canvas with the same number of threads per inch as the chart has squares per inch. With knitting and crocheting, the size will vary according to the number of stitches per inch.

COUNTED CROSS-STITCH

MATERIALS

1. **Needles.** A small blunt tapestry needle, No. 24 or No. 26.

2. **Fabric.** Evenweave linen, cotton, wool or synthetic fabrics all work well. The most popular fabrics are aida cloth, linen and hardanger cloth. Cotton aida is most commonly available in 18 threads-per-inch, 14 threads-per-inch and 11 threads-per-inch (14-count is the most popular size). Evenweave linen comes in a variety of threads-per-inch. To work cross-stitch on linen involves a slightly different technique (see page 4). Thirty thread-per-inch linen will result in a stitch about the same size as 14-count aida. Hardanger cloth has 22 threads to the inch and is available in cotton or linen. The amount of fabric needed depends on the size of the cross-stitch design. To determine yardage, divide the number of stitches in the design by the thread-count of the fabric. For example: If a design 42 squares wide by 70 squares deep is worked on a 14-count fabric, divide 42 by 14 (= 3), and 70 by 14 (= 5). The design will measure 3" × 5". The same design worked on 22-count fabric measures about 2" × 3¼".

3. **Threads and Yarns.** Six-strand embroidery floss, crewel wool, Danish Flower Thread, pearl cotton or metallic threads all work well for cross-stitch. DMC Embroidery Floss has been used to color-code the patterns in this volume. Crewel wool works well on evenweave wool fabric. Danish Flower Thread is a thicker thread with a matte finish, one strand equaling two of embroidery floss.

4. **Embroidery Hoop.** A wooden or plastic 4", 5" or 6" round or oval hoop with a screw-type tension adjuster works best for cross-stitch.

5. **Scissors.** A pair of sharp embroidery scissors is essential to all embroidery.

PREPARING TO WORK

To prevent raveling, either whip stitch or machine-stitch the outer edges of the fabric.

Locate the exact center of the chart (many of the charts in this book have arrows at the sides; follow these arrows to their intersection to locate the chart center). Establish the center of the fabric by folding it in half first vertically, then horizontally. The center stitch of the chart falls where the creases of the fabric meet. Mark the fabric center with a basting thread.

It is best to begin cross-stitch at the top of the design. To establish the top, count the squares up from the center of the chart, and the corresponding number of holes up from the center of the fabric.

Place the fabric tautly in the embroidery hoop, for tension makes it easier to push the needle through the holes without piercing the fibers. While working continue to retighten the fabric as necessary.

When working with multiple strands (such as embroidery floss) always separate (strand) the thread before beginning to stitch. This one small step allows for better coverage of the fabric. When you need more than one thread in the needle, use separate strands and do not double the thread. (For example: If you need four strands, use four separated strands.) Thread has a nap (just as fabrics do) and can be felt to be smoother in one direction than the other. Always work with the nap (the smooth side) pointing down.

For 14-count aida and 30-count linen, work with two strands of six-strand floss. For more texture, use more thread; for a flatter look, use less thread.

EMBROIDERY

To begin, fasten the thread with a waste knot and hold a short length of thread on the underside of the work, anchoring it with the first few stitches (*Diagram 1*). When the thread end is securely in place, clip the knot.

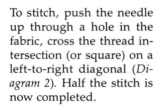

DIAGRAM 1
Reverse side of work

To stitch, push the needle up through a hole in the fabric, cross the thread intersection (or square) on a left-to-right diagonal (*Diagram 2*). Half the stitch is now completed.

DIAGRAM 2

Next, cross back, right to left, forming an X (*Diagram 3*).

DIAGRAM 3   DIAGRAM 4

Work all the same color stitches on one row, then cross back, completing the X's (*Diagram 4*).

Some needleworkers prefer to cross each stitch as they come to it. This method also works, but be sure all of the top stitches are slanted in the same direction. Isolated stitches must be crossed as they are worked. Vertical stitches are crossed as shown in *Diagram 5*.

DIAGRAM 5

At the top, work horizontal rows of a single color, left to right. This method allows you to go from an unoccupied space to an occupied space (working from an empty hole to a filled one), making ruffling of the floss less likely. Holes are used more than once, and all stitches "hold hands" unless a space is indicated on the chart. Hold the work upright throughout (do not turn as with many needlepoint stitches).

When carrying the thread from one area to another, run the needle under a few stitches on the wrong side. Do not carry thread across an open expanse of fabric as it will be visible from the front when the project is completed.

To end a color, weave in and out of the underside of the stitches, making a scallop stitch or two for extra security (*Diagram 6*). When possible, end in the same direction in which you were working, jumping up a row if necessary (*Diagram 7*). This prevents holes caused by stitches being pulled in two directions. Trim the thread ends closely and do not leave any tails or knots as they will show through the fabric when the work is completed.

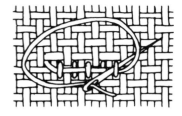

DIAGRAM 6
Reverse side of work

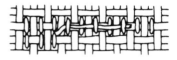

DIAGRAM 7
Reverse side of work

A number of other counted-thread stitches can be used in cross-stitch. Backstitch (*Diagram 8*) is used for outlines, face details and the like. It is worked from hole to hole, and may be stitched as a vertical, horizontal or diagonal line.

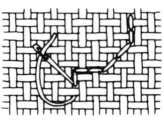

DIAGRAM 8

French knots (*Diagram 9*) are handy for special effects. They are worked in the same manner as on regular embroidery.

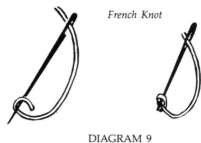

French Knot

DIAGRAM 9

Embroidery on Linen. Working on linen requires a slightly different technique. While evenweave linen is remarkably regular, there are always a few thick or thin threads. To keep the stitches even, cross-stitch is worked over two threads in each direction (*Diagram 10*).

DIAGRAM 10

As you are working over more threads, linen affords a greater variation in stitches. A half-stitch can slant in either direction and is uncrossed. A three-quarters stitch is shown in *Diagram 11*.

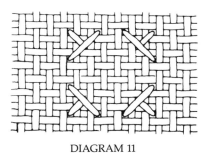

DIAGRAM 11

Embroidery on Gingham. Gingham and other checked fabrics can be used for cross-stitch. Using the fabric as a guide, work the stitches from corner to corner of each check.

Diagram 12 shows the backstitch worked on linen.

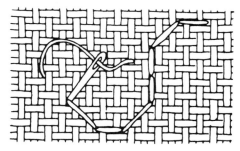

DIAGRAM 12

Embroidery on Uneven-Weave Fabrics. If you wish to work cross-stitch on an uneven-weave fabric, baste a lightweight Penelope needlepoint canvas to the material. The design can then be stitched by working the cross-stitch over the double mesh of the canvas. When working in this manner, take care not to catch the threads of the canvas in the embroidery. After the cross-stitch is completed, remove the basting threads. With tweezers remove first the vertical threads, one strand at a time, of the needlepoint canvas, then the horizontal threads.

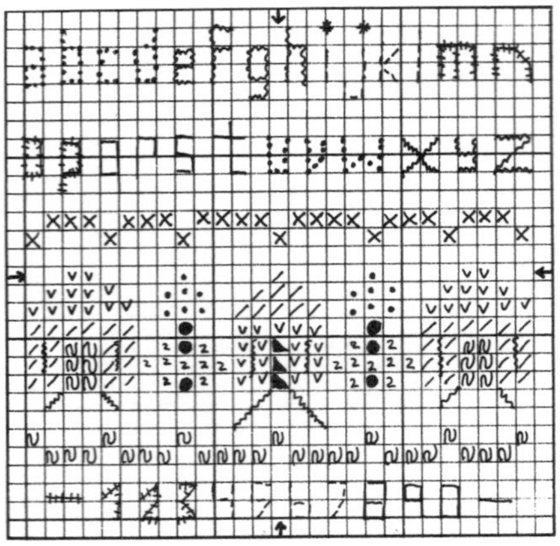

◄ HOUSES SAMPLER

French Knot	Back-stitch	Cross-stitch	DMC#	
		Z	503	Medium Blue Green
	····	∾	958	Dark Aqua
	——	◣	517	Medium Wedgwood Blue
		V	760	Salmon
✱	- - -	☒	817	Very Dark Coral Red
		⁄	733	Medium Olive Green
	~~	●	829	Dark Avocado Leaf Green
	++++		904	Very Dark Parrot Green
		·	907	Light Parrot Green

OVAL SAMPLER ►

Back-stitch	Cross-stitch	DMC#	
~~	⊞	209	Dark Lavender
oooo	◣	221	Dark Pinkish Brown
——	☒	518	Light Wedgwood Blue
•—•—•	·	725	Topaz
═══	∾	894	Very Light Carnation
••••	—	3340	Melon
~~	●	3346	Hunter Green
- - -	⁄	3348	Light Yellow Green

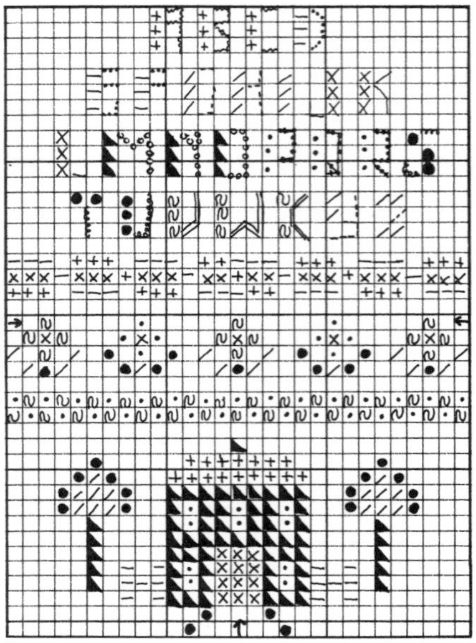

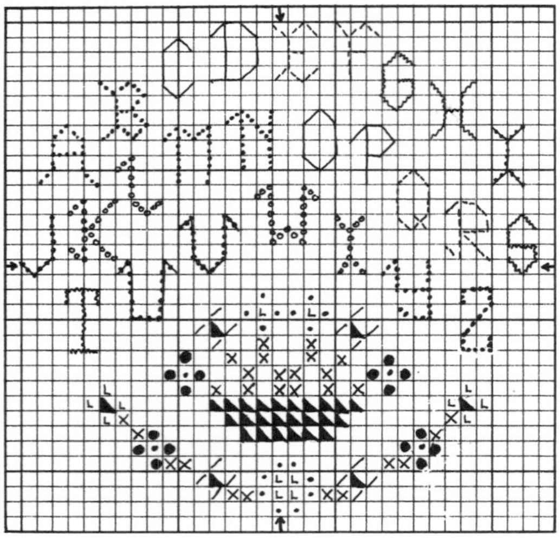

◄ ROUND SAMPLER

Back-stitch	Cross-stitch	DMC#	
•—•—•	⁄	223	Pinkish Brown
~~	◣	597	Turquoise
- - -	·	726	Light Topaz
••••	L	776	Medium Pink
——	☒	906	Medium Parrot Green
oooo	●	3340	Melon

BEST WISHES ►

Back-stitch	Cross-stitch	DMC#	
	⁄	471	Light Avocado Green
——		700	Bright Christmas Green
	●	958	Dark Aqua
	∾	900	Dark Burnt Orange
	I	970	Light Pumpkin
	·	972	Yellow Orange

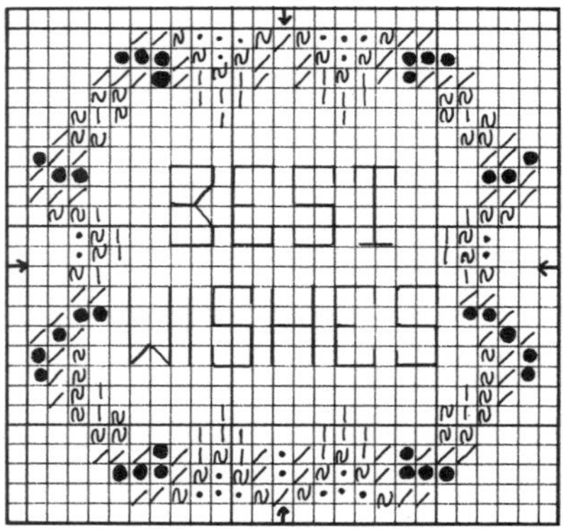

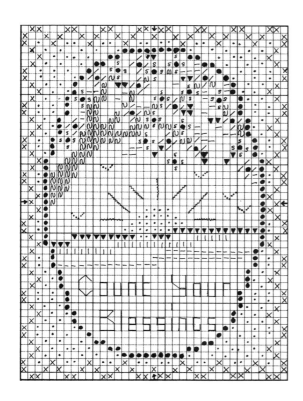

◄ **COUNT YOUR BLESSINGS**

Back-stitch	Cross-stitch	DMC#	
	Ⓢ	352	Light Coral
•••••	☑	602	Medium Cranberry
	Ⓝ	433	Medium Brown
———		700	Bright Christmas Green
	Ⓘ	703	Chartreuse
	▼	905	Dark Parrot Green
	⊟	907	Light Parrot Green
〜〜	⊡	741	Medium Tangerine
	●	798	Dark Delft Blue
	☒	809	Delft Blue

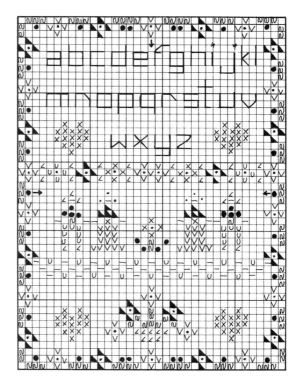

HEARTS SAMPLER ►

French Knot	Back-stitch	Cross-stitch	DMC#	
		☒	349	Dark Coral
		⊟	353	Peach
		●	471	Light Avocado Green
		Ⓝ	3346	Hunter Green
		▼	740	Tangerine
		⊡	743	Dark Yellow
		◣	947	Burnt Orange
✳	———	Ⓤ	826	Medium Blue
		◿	833	Medium Golden Wheat

◄ **LOVE ONE ANOTHER**

Back-stitch	Cross-stitch	DMC#	
———		400	Dark Mahogany
	●	606	Bright Orange Red
	☒	3706	Medium Watermelon
〜〜〜		703	Chartreuse
	Ⓘ	907	Light Parrot Green
	⊡	726	Topaz

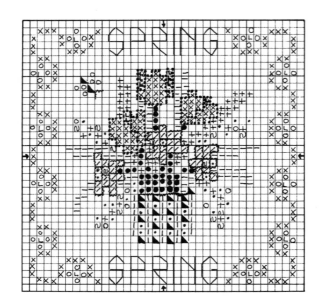

◄ SPRING

Back-stitch	Cross-stitch	DMC #	
	⊡	407	Medium Cocoa Brown
∼∼∼	◣	632	Chocolate Brown
·····		550	Very Dark Violet
	L	553	Medium Violet
	⊠	554	Light Violet
———	⊙	603	Cranberry
	●	700	Bright Christmas Green
	⊞	702	Kelly Green
	⊟	704	Bright Chartreuse
	⊿	742	Light Tangerine
	◈	947	Burnt Orange
	·	3341	Light Melon

SUMMER ►

Back-stitch	Cross-stitch	DMC #	
	⊟	892	Medium Carnation
	⊡	742	Light Tangerine
	·	973	Bright Canary Yellow
	◈	947	Burnt Orange
∼∼∼	●	918	Dark Red Copper
	⊙	920	Medium Copper
	L	922	Light Copper
———	⊞	910	Dark Emerald Green
	◣	912	Light Emerald Green
	⊿	954	Nile Green

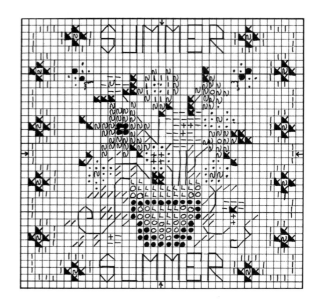

◄ AUTUMN

Back-stitch	Cross-stitch	DMC #	
	⊟	321	Christmas Red
	◣	815	Medium Garnet Red
	⊠	721	Bittersweet
	·	742	Light Tangerine
	⊡	946	Medium Burnt Orange
	●	904	Very Dark Parrot Green
	L	907	Light Parrot Green
····	◈	975	Dark Golden Brown
———		976	Medium Golden Brown
∼∼∼	⊙	3045	Dark Yellow Beige

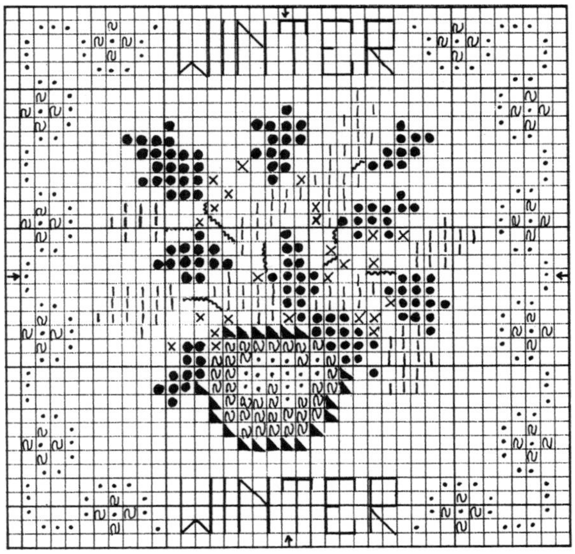

◄ WINTER

Back-stitch	Cross-stitch	DMC#	
	◣	517	Medium Wedgwood Blue
——	∾	518	Light Wedgwood Blue
	⊡	519	Sky Blue
	☒	666	Bright Christmas Red
	◫	320	Medium Pistachio Green
〰	●	3345	Dark Hunter Green

BE HAPPY ►

Cross-stitch	DMC#	
⊡	209	Dark Lavender
●	550	Very Dark Violet
∾	349	Dark Coral
☒	604	Light Cranberry

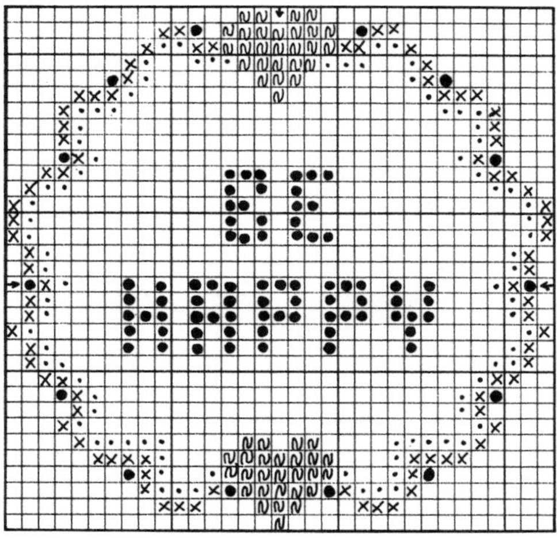

WHEN ONE DOOR CLOSES ▼

Back-stitch	Cross-stitch	DMC#	
	☑	825	Dark Blue
	●	906	Medium Parrot Green
——	∾	920	Medium Copper
	⧄	3340	Melon

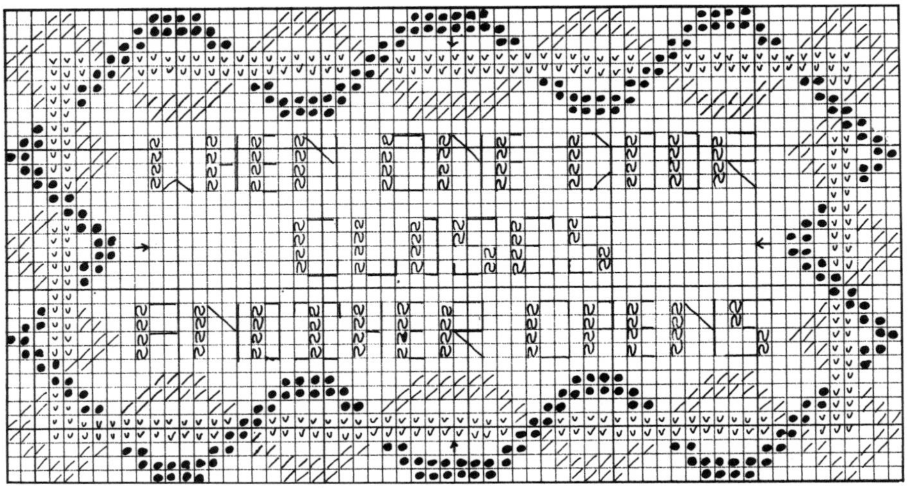

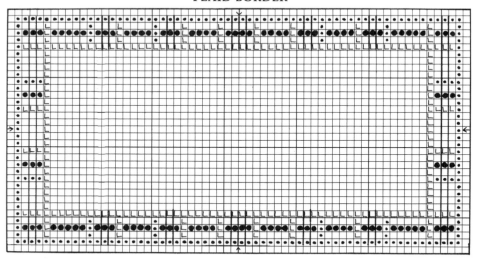

PLAID BORDER

CLASSIC MONOGRAM
WITH TWO BORDERS

Back-stitch	Cross-stitch	DMC#	
	●	311	Medium Navy Blue
	L	931	Medium Antique Blue
	V	918	Dark Red Copper
──	N	919	Red Copper
	·	922	Light Copper

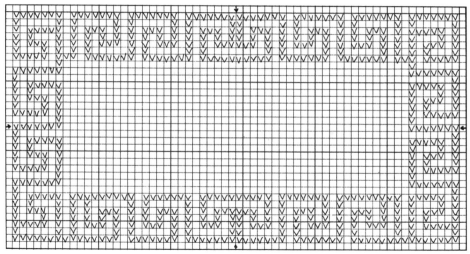

GREEK KEY BORDER

▲ HOMES ARE OF LOVE

Back-stitch	Cross-stitch	DMC #	
	☑	209	Dark Lavender
——	⋂	552	Dark Violet
	·	604	Light Cranberry
	●	666	Bright Christmas Red
	▲	741	Medium Tangerine
	☑	907	Light Parrot Green

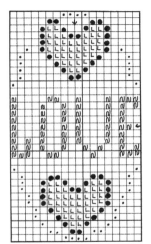

LOVE ▶

Cross-stitch	DMC #	
●	304	Medium Christmas Red
L	666	Bright Christmas Red
·	907	Light Parrot Green
⋂	943	Medium Aquamarine

▲ WHAT ARE LITTLE GIRLS MADE OF?

French Knot	Back-stitch	Cross-stitch	DMC#		French Knot	Back-stitch	Cross-stitch	DMC#	
	〜〜	⊞	604	Light Cranberry			⊘	799	Medium Delft Blue
		⊡	726	Light Topaz	o	—	◉	904	Very Dark Parrot Green
▫	- - - -	➡	729	Medium Old Gold			⊟	906	Medium Parrot Green
		▼	972	Yellow Orange			☑	907	Light Parrot Green
		▲	754	Light Peach		.....	⑅	3705	Watermelon
✳		⑤	798	Dark Delft Blue					

▼ HOME IS WHERE THE HEART IS

Cross-stitch	DMC#	
◉	347	Dark Salmon
⑅	3328	Medium Salmon
⊘	760	Salmon
☒	606	Bright Orange Red
⑃	959	Aqua

WHAT ARE LITTLE BOYS MADE OF? ▲

French Knot	Back-stitch	Cross-stitch	DMC#	
✳	〜〜	☒	400	Dark Mahogany
		■	754	Light Peach
		⊡	726	Light Topaz
×	—		797	Royal Blue
		⑃	798	Dark Delft Blue
		⊘	799	Medium Delft Blue
▫	- - - -	◉	904	Very Dark Parrot Green
		⊟	905	Dark Parrot Green
		☑	907	Light Parrot Green
		⑅	3705	Watermelon

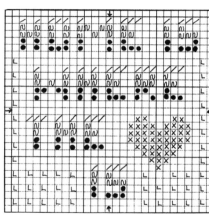

MOTHER'S DAY ▶

Back-stitch	Cross-stitch	DMC #	
	⊡	605	Very Light Cranberry
	☒	704	Bright Chartreuse
——		995	Dark Electric Blue

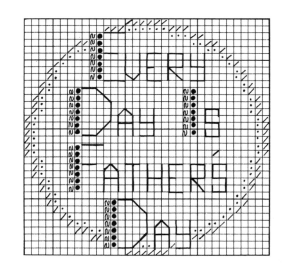

◀ TOMORROW IS A BRIGHT NEW DAY

Back-stitch	Cross-stitch	DMC #	
V		300	Very Dark Mahogany
——		347	Dark Salmon
	☒	741	Medium Tangerine
∿∿		946	Medium Burnt Orange
	⊡	964	Light Aqua

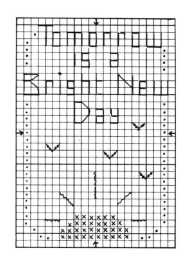

FATHER'S DAY ▶

Back-stitch	Cross-stitch	DMC #	
	⊡	676	Light Old Gold
	☑	680	Dark Old Gold
——	⬤	797	Royal Blue
	⋈	799	Medium Delft Blue

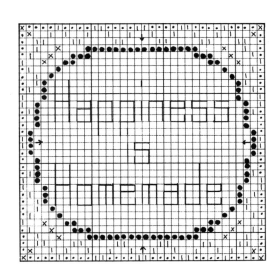

◀ HAPPINESS IS HOMEMADE

Back-stitch	Cross-stitch	DMC #	
——		400	Dark Mahogany
	⬤	517	Medium Wedgwood Blue
	⊡	519	Sky Blue
	☒	913	Medium Nile Green
	⊓	3608	Fuchsia

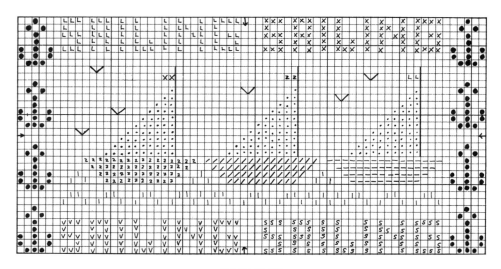

▲ SAILING

Back-stitch	Cross-stitch	DMC#	
●		434	Light Brown
——		976	Medium Golden Brown
	⊞	519	Sky Blue
	☒	807	Peacock Blue
	⊘	604	Light Cranberry
	⊡	702	Kelly Green
	⑤	704	Bright Chartreuse
	☒	947	Burnt Orange
	⊟	970	Light Pumpkin
	⊡	973	Bright Canary Yellow
	☑	3705	Watermelon

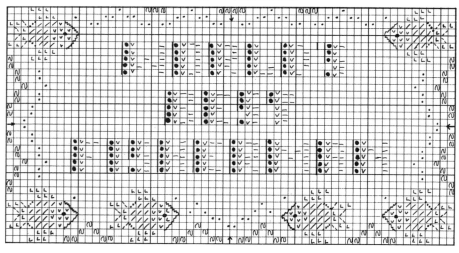

▲ WORLD'S BEST FISHERMAN

French Knot	Back-stitch	Cross-stitch	DMC#	
	- - - -	⊡	704	Bright Chartreuse
○	——		943	Medium Aquamarine
		ℕ	958	Dark Aqua
		⊡	964	Light Aqua
		⊟	970	Light Pumpkin
	∿∿∿	☑	972	Yellow Orange
	‧‧‧‧‧	⊘	973	Bright Canary Yellow
		●	976	Medium Golden Brown

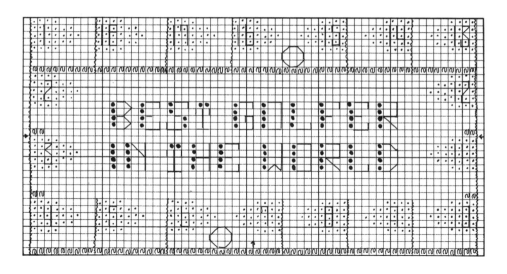

BEST GOLFER ▲

Back-stitch	Cross-stitch	DMC#	
~~		433	Medium Brown
	·	666	Bright Christmas Red
	₪	702	Kelly Green
———	●	797	Royal Blue

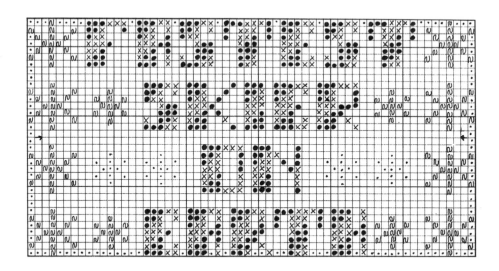

FASTEST SKIER ▲

Cross-stitch	DMC#	
●	349	Dark Coral
✕	351	Coral
₪	823	Dark Navy Blue
·	827	Very Light Blue

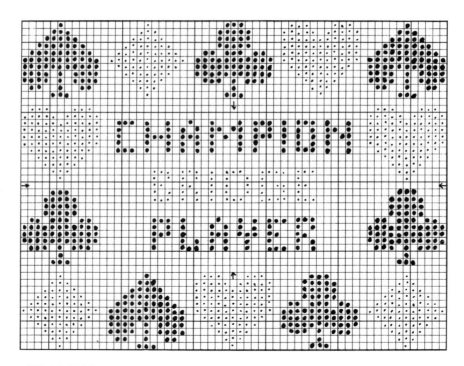

CHAMPION BRIDGE PLAYER ▲

Cross-stitch	DMC#	
◉	310	Black
⊡	666	Bright Christmas Red

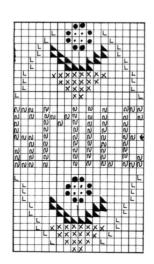

SMILE ▶

Back-stitch	Cross-stitch	DMC#	
	◉	321	Christmas Red
	⊡	444	Dark Lemon Yellow
——	◼	701	Light Christmas Green
	⌊	704	Bright Chartreuse
	☒	920	Medium Copper
	∾	946	Medium Burnt Orange

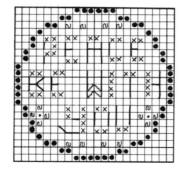

◀ PEACE BE WITH YOU

Back-stitch	Cross-stitch	DMC#	
	◉	517	Medium Wedgwood Blue
——		518	Light Wedgwood Blue
∿∿	☒	519	Sky Blue
	⊡	745	Light Yellow
	∾	957	Pale Geranium Pink

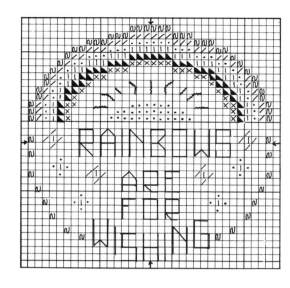

◄ **RAINBOWS ARE FOR WISHING**

Back-stitch	Cross-stitch	DMC #	
	☒	208	Very Dark Lavender
	⋈	666	Bright Christmas Green
	Ⅱ	703	Chartreuse
——	◼	826	Medium Blue
～～	⧄	970	Light Pumpkin
	·	973	Bright Canary Yellow

▼ **CONGRATULATIONS**

Back-stitch	Cross-stitch	DMC #	
	⧄	340	Lilac
	▲	553	Medium Violet
～～	⧄	436	Tan
	⋈	606	Bright Orange Red
	▽	740	Tangerine
	·	742	Light Tangerine
	◼	817	Very Dark Coral Red
	◉	703	Chartreuse
——		798	Dark Delft Blue
	☒	813	Light Blue
	Ⅱ	995	Dark Electric Blue
	⊟	959	Aqua
	⧄	3607	Dark Fuchsia

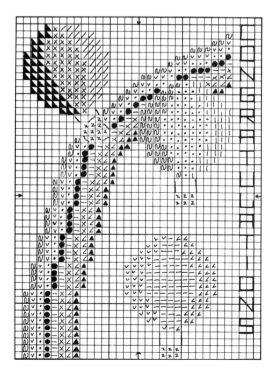

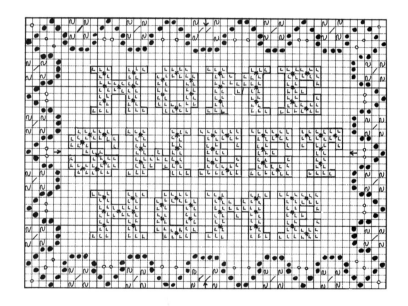

HOME SWEET HOME ▲

French Knot	Back-stitch	Cross-stitch	DMC #	
		⧄	309	Deep Rose
		⋈	894	Very Light Carnation Pink
○			742	Light Tangerine
✳	——		797	Royal Blue
		L	799	Medium Delft Blue
		◉	906	Medium Parrot Green

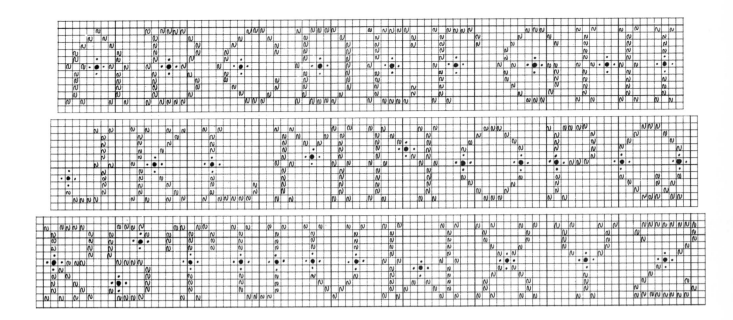

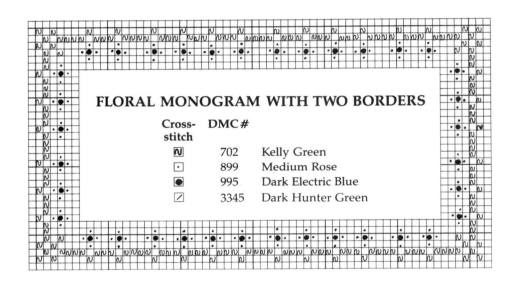

FLORAL MONOGRAM WITH TWO BORDERS

Cross-stitch	DMC #	
⑅	702	Kelly Green
⋅	899	Medium Rose
●	995	Dark Electric Blue
╱	3345	Dark Hunter Green

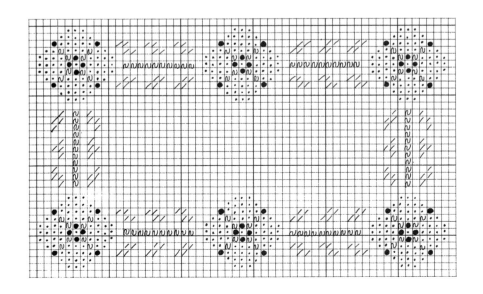

BE MY VALENTINE ▶

Back-stitch	Cross-stitch	DMC #	
⊡		471	Light Avocado Green
⋈		704	Bright Chartreuse
——		517	Medium Wedgwood Blue
∿∿	◉	666	Bright Christmas Red
	⊘	3706	Medium Watermelon

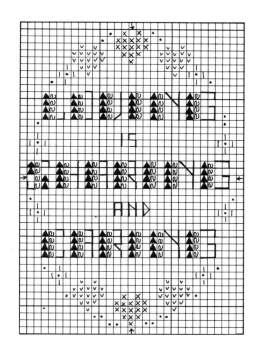

◀ LOVING IS SHARING AND CARING

Back-stitch	Cross-stitch	DMC #	
	☒	606	Bright Orange Red
	☑	608	Bright Orange
	⊡	3341	Light Melon
	▲	702	Kelly Green
——	⋈	704	Bright Chartreuse
	⊡	973	Bright Canary Yellow

LOVE-ENJOY-HAPPY-LAUGH ▶

Back-stitch	Cross-stitch	DMC #	
	◉	356	Medium Terra-Cotta
	⊡	970	Light Pumpkin
	⊡	605	Very Light Cranberry
	⋈	666	Bright Christmas Red
	☒	702	Kelly Green
——		825	Dark Blue
	L	996	Medium Electric Blue

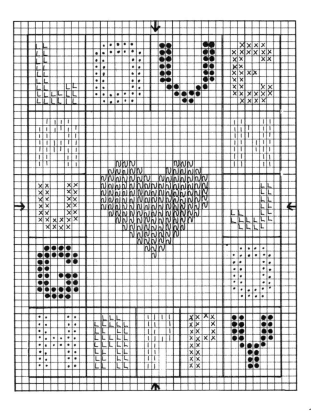

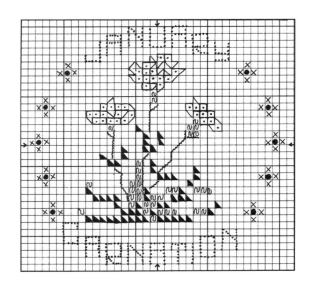

◄ JANUARY

Back-stitch	Cross-stitch	DMC #	
	☒	353	Peach
∿	◣	367	Dark Pistachio Green
	⋈	368	Light Pistachio Green
.....		553	Medium Violet
——	●	601	Dark Cranberry
	⊡	605	Very Light Cranberry

FEBRUARY ►

Back-stitch	Cross-stitch	DMC #	
••••		322	Light Marine Blue
	⋈	444	Dark Lemon Yellow
	▲	550	Very Dark Violet
⌇⌇⌇	●	552	Dark Violet
	⊡	554	Light Violet
——		562	Sea Foam Green
	⊟	563	Medium Sea Foam Green
∿		564	Light Sea Foam Green
	☒	3708	Light Watermelon

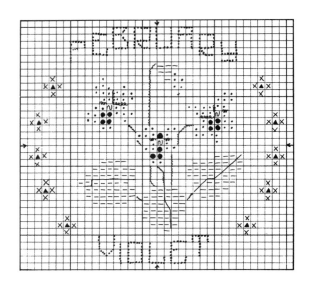

◄ MARCH

French Knot	Back-stitch	Cross-stitch	DMC #	
		ⓩ	740	Tangerine
		⌶	742	Light Tangerine
		⊡	973	Bright Canary Yellow
	——		780	Very Dark Topaz
		●	783	Christmas Gold
		⋈	807	Peacock Blue
		⊟	911	Medium Emerald Green
✳		☒	912	Light Emerald Green
	∿		918	Dark Red Copper

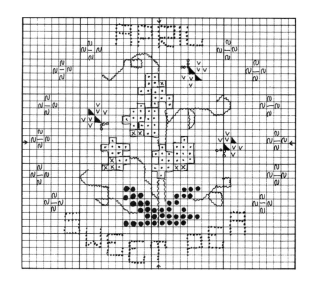

APRIL ▶

Back-stitch	Cross-stitch	DMC #	
oooo	◣	436	Tan
	☑	444	Dark Lemon Yellow
	И	603	Cranberry
——		718	Plum
	—	917	Medium Plum
	·	3608	Fuchsia
	☒	3708	Light Watermelon
	◉	700	Bright Christmas Green
.....		702	Kelly Green
~~		703	Chartreuse

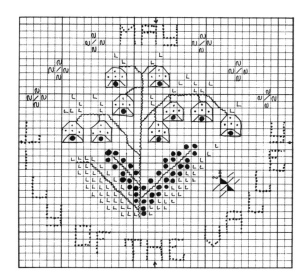

◀ MAY

Back-stitch	Cross-stitch	DMC #	
ooooo	◣	436	Tan
——		3023	Light Brown Gray
	◸	444	Dark Lemon Yellow
	ㄴ	471	Light Avocado Green
	◉	469	Avocado Green
~~		937	Medium Avocado Green
	И	553	Medium Violet
.....		603	Cranberry
	·		White

JUNE ▶

Back-stitch	Cross-stitch	DMC #	
	—	307	Lemon Yellow
	☒	444	Dark Lemon Yellow
	Ⓢ	741	Medium Tangerine
——	▲	309	Deep Rose
	И	899	Medium Rose
	·	776	Medium Pink
ooooo	◉	436	Tan
~~		701	Light Christmas Green
	☑	703	Chartreuse
.....		996	Medium Electric Blue

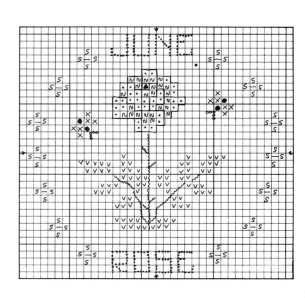

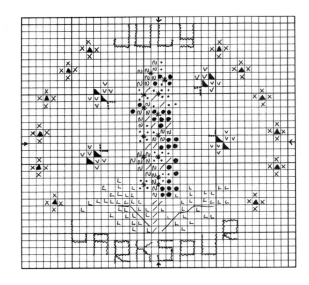

French Knot	Back-stitch	Cross-stitch	DMC #	
✳	∼∼∼		208	Very Dark Lavender
		☑	444	Dark Lemon Yellow
	.....	◣	436	Tan
		●	602	Medium Cranberry
		ᴎ	603	Cranberry
		·	605	Very Light Cranberry
		☒	606	Bright Orange Red
	——	╱	702	Kelly Green
		L	704	Bright Chartreuse
		▲	3708	Light Watermelon

AUGUST ►

Back-stitch	Cross-stitch	DMC #	
	☒	349	Dark Coral
	·	352	Light Coral
∼∼∼		355	Dark Terra-Cotta
——		498	Dark Christmas Red
	●	815	Medium Garnet Red
.....	◣	436	Tan
	☑	444	Dark Lemon
	Ⅰ	970	Light Pumpkin
	⑤	972	Yellow Orange
	ᴎ	905	Dark Parrot Green
	⊟	907	Light Parrot Green

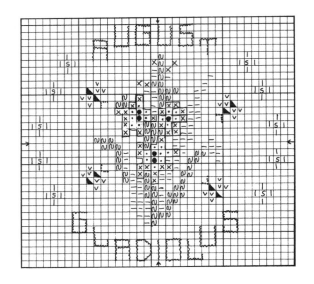

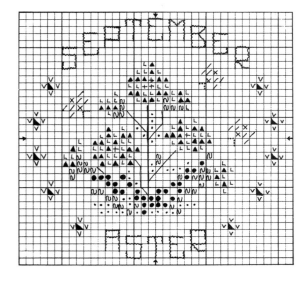

Back-stitch	Cross-stitch	DMC #	
	▲	208	Very Dark Lavender
	L	210	Medium Lavender
.....	☒	436	Tan
	◣	976	Medium Golden Brown
	╱	444	Dark Lemon Yellow
∼∼∼	⊞	740	Tangerine
	☑	947	Burnt Orange
	●	905	Dark Parrot Green
——	ᴎ	906	Medium Parrot Green
	·	907	Light Parrot Green

OCTOBER ▶

Back-stitch	Cross-stitch	DMC #	
	◉	701	Light Christmas Green
	U	702	Kelly Green
	·	704	Bright Chartreuse
	N	725	Topaz
	S	742	Light Tangerine
	V	743	Dark Yellow
	Z	783	Christmas Gold
	▲	900	Dark Burnt Orange
	X	947	Burnt Orange
———		920	Medium Copper
∿∿∿		975	Dark Golden Brown

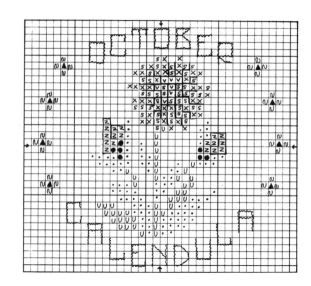

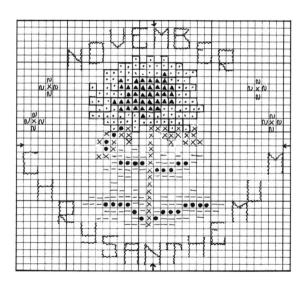

◀ NOVEMBER

Back-stitch	Cross-stitch	DMC #	
	◉	319	Very Dark Pistachio Green
	X	367	Dark Pistachio Green
	—	368	Light Pistachio Green
	N	722	Medium Bittersweet
	·	740	Tangerine
∿∿∿		900	Dark Burnt Orange
	▲	947	Burnt Orange
———		918	Dark Red Copper

DECEMBER ▶

Back-stitch	Cross-stitch	DMC #	
∿∿∿	◉	666	Bright Christmas Red
———	N	904	Very Dark Parrot Green
	⧄	906	Medium Parrot Green
	◣	995	Dark Electric Blue
	·	996	Medium Electric Blue

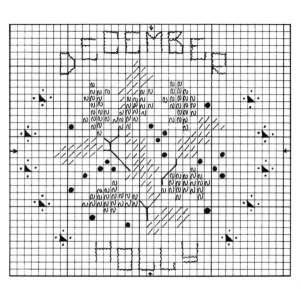

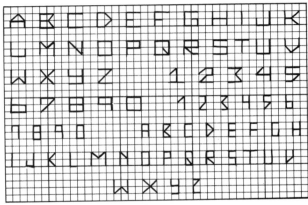

ALPHABET FOR PERSONALIZING SAMPLERS
Work in backstitch in color desired.

◄ HAPPY ANNIVERSARY

Back-stitch	Cross-stitch	DMC #	
～～～	◉	517	Medium Wedgwood Blue
	L	518	Light Wedgwood Blue
	╱	519	Sky Blue
	Ⴂ	892	Medium Carnation Pink
——	·	3708	Light Watermelon

For number, use chart above, working each stitch over 2 threads rather than 1.

WEDDING SAMPLER ►

Back-stitch	Cross-stitch	DMC #	
～～～		352	Light Coral
.....	Ⴂ	606	Bright Orange Red
	⊡	740	Tangerine
	·	973	Bright Canary Yellow
	☒	603	Cranberry
	☑	784	Very Dark Cornflower Blue
——	◉	797	Royal Blue
	╱	996	Medium Electric Blue
	⊟	912	Light Emerald Green
	·	964	Light Aqua

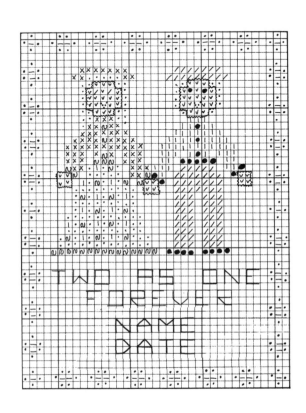

◄ GRADUATION

Back-stitch	Cross-stitch	DMC #	
——	●	310	Black
∼∼∼	X	433	Medium Brown
	C	435	Very Light Brown
	I	437	Light Tan
· · · ·	▲	975	Dark Golden Brown
	∕	976	Medium Golden Brown
	S	977	Light Golden Brown
	■	444	Dark Lemon Yellow
– – – –		701	Light Christmas Green
	ᴎ	702	Kelly Green
	–	907	Light Parrot Green
	V	809	Delft Blue

▼ BUTTERFLY SAMPLER

Back-stitch	Cross-stitch	DMC #	
	ᴎ	315	Dark Antique Mauve
∼∼∼		322	Light Marine Blue
——		336	Navy Blue
	X	351	Coral
	■	3341	Light Melon
	L	368	Light Pistachio Green
	·	676	Light Old Gold
· · · · ·	●	975	Dark Golden Brown

BABIES TOUCH THE WORLD WITH LOVE ▼

French Knot	Back-stitch	Cross-stitch	DMC #	
		V	604	Light Cranberry
		ᴎ	702	Kelly Green
		∕	704	Bright Chartreuse
		·	741	Medium Tangerine
o	——		996	Medium Electric Blue

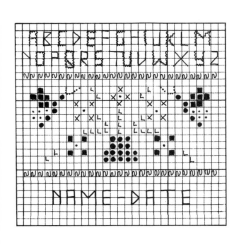

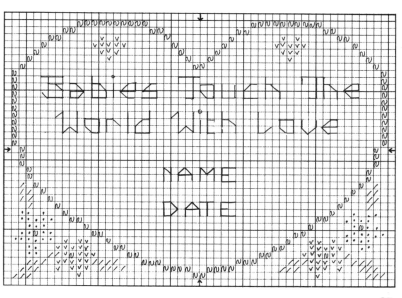

LET A SMILE BE YOUR UMBRELLA ▶

French Knot	Back-stitch	Cross-stitch	DMC #	
		●	597	Turquoise
		V	598	Light Turquoise
	～～	N	632	Chocolate Brown
		╱	666	Bright Christmas Red
		⊟	703	Chartreuse
		·	972	Yellow Orange
✳	———	◣	995	Dark Electric Blue

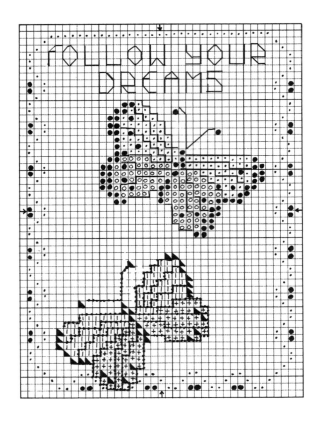

◀ FOLLOW YOUR DREAMS

Back-stitch	Cross-stitch	DMC #	
	⊙	598	Light Turquoise
	●	806	Dark Peacock Blue
	·	807	Peacock Blue
———		824	Very Dark Blue
•-•-•-•	◣	900	Dark Burnt Orange
	N	970	Light Pumpkin
	⊓	972	Yellow Orange
	⊞	973	Bright Canary Yellow

I LOVE YOU ▶

Back-stitch	Cross-stitch	DMC #	
～～	N	606	Bright Orange Red
·····	⊠	703	Chartreuse
●●●●	·	972	Yellow Orange
———	●	996	Medium Electric Blue

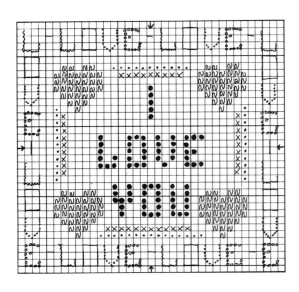

MULTICOLORED MONOGRAM
WITH TWO BORDERS

Cross-stitch	DMC#	
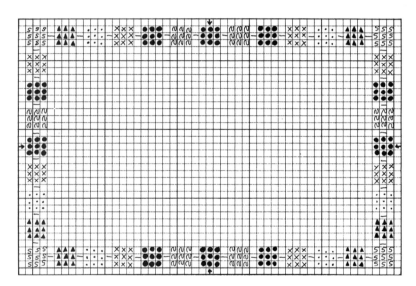	518	Light Wedgwood Blue
●	826	Medium Blue
⌐	813	Light Blue
Ⓝ	553	Medium Violet
⁄	605	Very Light Cranberry
S	606	Bright Orange Red
⊟	608	Bright Orange
▼	970	Light Pumpkin
·	972	Yellow Orange
⊓	3341	Light Melon
Z	703	Chartreuse
X	704	Bright Chartreuse
∧	907	Light Parrot Green

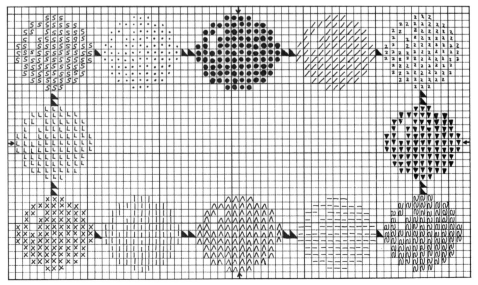

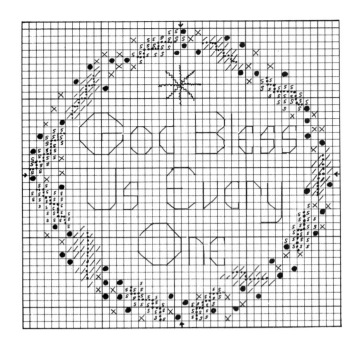

◄ **GOD BLESS US EVERY ONE**

Back-stitch	Cross-stitch	DMC #	
	◖	498	Dark Christmas Red
	☒	666	Bright Christmas Red
〰		972	Yellow Orange
⋯⋯		905	Dark Parrot Green
	S	906	Medium Parrot Green
	⟋	907	Light Parrot Green
────		995	Dark Electric Blue

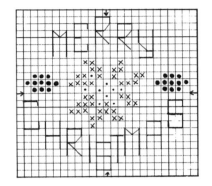

▲ **MERRY CHRISTMAS**

Back-stitch	Cross-stitch	DMC #	
	⊡	444	Dark Lemon Yellow
	☒	666	Bright Christmas Red
────		701	Light Christmas Green
	◉	703	Chartreuse

▼ **SEASON'S GREETINGS**

Back-stitch	Cross-stitch	DMC #	
	☒	666	Bright Christmas Red
	◉	700	Bright Christmas Green
	⊡	703	Chartreuse
────	∾		Metallic Gold

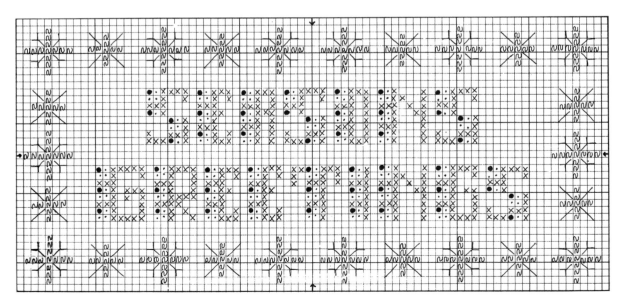

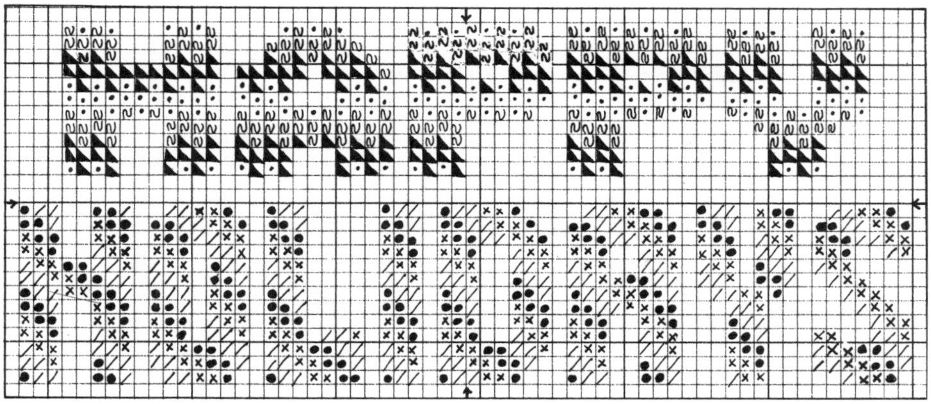

HAPPY HOLIDAYS ▲

Cross-stitch	DMC#	
N	606	Bright Orange Red
·	608	Bright Orange
◣	817	Very Dark Coral Red
●	909	Very Dark Emerald Green
✕	911	Medium Emerald Green
/	913	Medium Nile Green

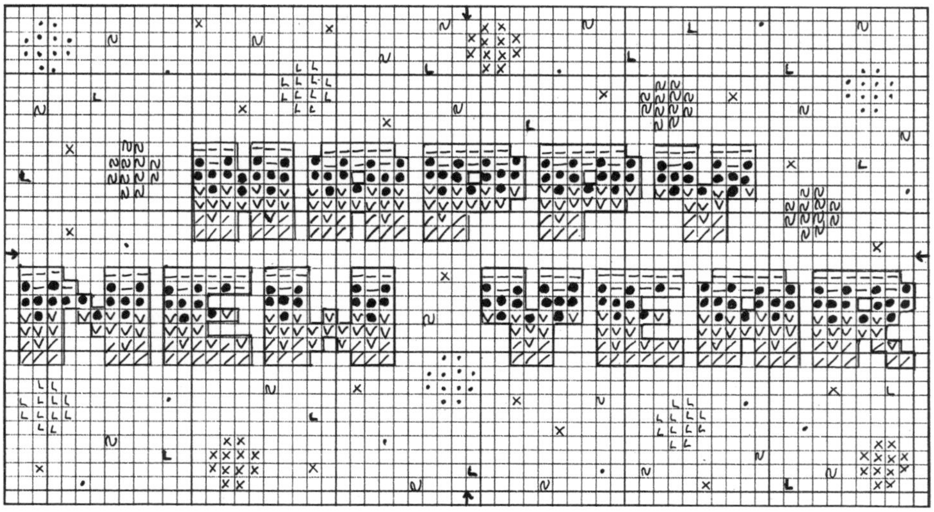

HAPPY NEW YEAR ▲

Back-stitch	Cross-stitch	DMC#	
	L	519	Sky Blue
	●	996	Medium Electric Blue
——		798	Dark Delft Blue
	✕	608	Bright Orange
	−	666	Bright Christmas Red
	·	743	Dark Yellow
	V	972	Yellow Orange
	/	702	Kelly Green
	N	704	Bright Chartreuse

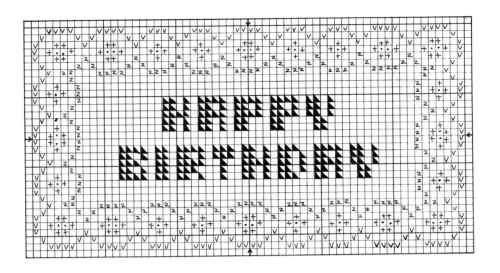

▲ FLORAL BIRTHDAY GREETINGS

Cross-stitch	DMC #	
◣	355	Dark Terra-Cotta
✚	760	Salmon
⊡	444	Dark Lemon Yellow
Z	825	Dark Blue
V	913	Medium Nile Green

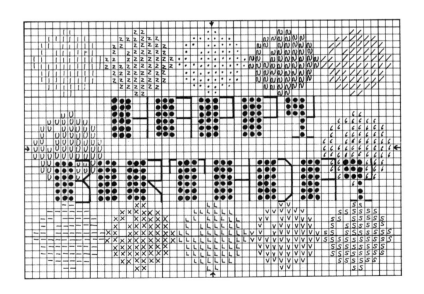

▲ BIRTHDAY BALLOONS

Back-stitch	Cross-stitch	DMC #		Cross-stitch	DMC #	
	U	210	Medium Lavender	L	742	Light Tangerine
———	●	517	Medium Wedgwood Blue	I	726	Light Topaz
	V	519	Sky Blue	6	907	Light Parrot Green
	Z	964	Light Aqua	X	704	Bright Chartreuse
	⊟	603	Cranberry	N	913	Medium Nile Green
	⊡	606	Bright Orange Red	S	3708	Light Watermelon
	Z	740	Tangerine			

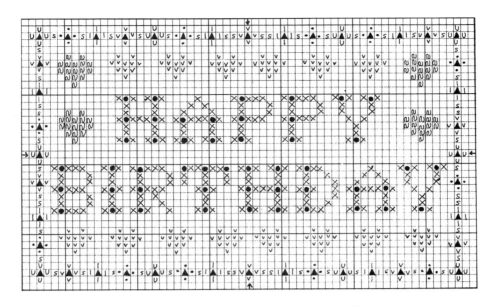

▲ HAPPY BIRTHDAY HEARTS

Cross-stitch	DMC #	
∪	209	Dark Lavender
✕	517	Medium Wedgwood Blue
●	518	Light Wedgwood Blue
Ⅰ	519	Sky Blue
∨	603	Cranberry

Cross-stitch	DMC #	
Ͷ	666	Bright Christmas Red
▲	702	Kelly Green
S	704	Bright Chartreuse
·	740	Tangerine

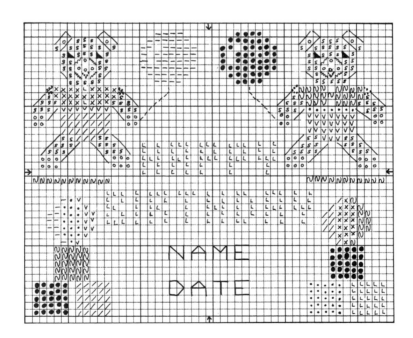

▲ TEDDY BEAR BIRTHDAY GREETINGS

Back-stitch	Cross-stitch	DMC #	
– – – –	∕	209	Dark Lavender
	◣	310	Black
	·	444	Dark Lemon Yellow
......	Ͷ	606	Bright Orange Red
	–	740	Tangerine
ᴑᴑᴑᴑᴑ	✕	3341	Light Melon

Back-stitch	Cross-stitch	DMC #	
	◉	703	Chartreuse
	∨	827	Very Light Blue
	L	996	Medium Electric Blue
———	S	975	Dark Golden Brown
∼∼∼	○	977	Light Golden Brown

Use alphabet on page 24 for name and date.

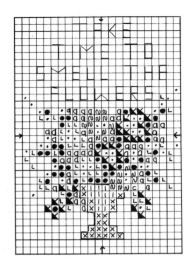

◄ TAKE TIME TO SMELL THE FLOWERS

Back-stitch	Cross-stitch	DMC #	
	·	444	Dark Lemon Yellow
	L	741	Medium Tangerine
——		700	Bright Christmas Green
	●	703	Chartreuse
	◪	912	Light Emerald Green
	☒	806	Dark Peacock Blue
	Ⅱ	807	Peacock Blue
	ℕ	3326	Light Rose
	◤	3705	Watermelon

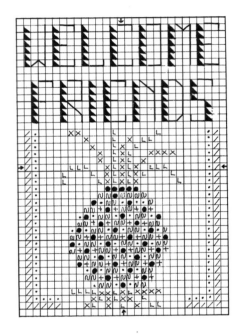

WELCOME FRIENDS ►

Back-stitch	Cross-stitch	DMC #	
	●	400	Dark Mahogany
	◣	580	Dark Moss Green
——	☒	701	Light Christmas Green
	◿	702	Kelly Green
	L	907	Light Parrot Green
	⊞	608	Bright Orange
	ℕ	970	Light Pumpkin
	·	973	Bright Canary Yellow

◄ A FRIEND IS A JOY FOREVER

Back-stitch	Cross-stitch	DMC #	
——		700	Bright Christmas Green
	●	703	Chartreuse
	·	742	Light Tangerine
	☒	947	Burnt Orange
	ℕ	894	Very Light Carnation Pink